MEDITATIONS
FOR
BEREAVED PARENTS

edited by
Judy Osgood

GILGAL PUBLICATIONS
P.O. Box 3399
Sunriver, Oregon 97707 USA
(503) 593-8418 Fax: (503) 593-5604

Library of Congress Cataloging-in-Publication Data

Meditations for bereaved parents.

    (Gilgal meditation series)
    1. Parents—Prayer-books and devotions—English.
    2. Bereavement—Religious aspects—Christianity—
Meditations. I. Osgood, Judy. II. Series.
BV4907.M39 1986   248.8'6   86-15003
ISBN 0-916895-00-9 (pbk.)

Printed in the United States of America.

Other books in the Gilgal Meditation Series:

MEDITATIONS FOR THE WIDOWED

MEDITATIONS FOR THE DIVORCED

**MEDITATIONS FOR THE TERMINALLY ILL
AND THEIR FAMILIES**

**MEDITATIONS FOR ALCOHOLICS
AND THEIR FAMILIES**

CONTENTS

IN MEMORY OF OUR CHILDREN

WHEN THE CYGNETS DIED

Can a mother forget the baby at her breast and have no compassion on the child she has borne? Though she may forget, I will not forget you!

Isaiah 49:15 (NIV)

I knew a long time ahead that I was going to have to live without Joey, and I knew what my strength would be - living with God. God Himself would hold me close and wipe away my tears. He would be "near to comfort and cheer" just when I needed Him most.

And then Joey died, and God died, too. For month after month after month He failed to touch the events in my life, without or within. Nor did the stories of God's special moments in the lives of other parents who had lost children help, for I had lost not only my son but my Father as well.

And then one day I read a story about a man and woman on the shores of Long Island Sound who befriended two symphonically beautiful swans, cautiously and joyously nourishing the friendship until the wild creatures would respond to their call, come up on their lawn and eat bread from their hands. The couple's awareness of the swans grew through the changing seasons, especially through the mating season and the appearance of the young cygnets.

The second year only strengthened the relationship until, upon the birth of the new swanlets, great black gulls swooped into the inlet and one by one seized and killed the pitifully screaming babes. Now the mother and father refused to answer the call of their friends, preferring to swim up the river again and again to the bridge where the last baby had been taken, or spending their days building a new nest, a nest that would never be filled. On occasion when they did wander up on their friends' lawn, they were too bewildered, too pre-occupied, to eat the bread held out to them.

The couple on the shore cursed nature, plotted revenge on the black gulls, shouted their love to the swans, bore the pain of the swan's inability to accept their love, and waited for another year. Never were the friends more present to their swans than when to the swans they appeared more absent.

And so, without inner signal or outer sign, I affirmed God's shouts of love to me, and in my deafest hour found the beginnings of comfort. And I, too, waited for another year.

Dear Father-Mother God, help me always to know that as much as I loved the child I lost, so much do you love me, and unimaginably more.

Meg Woodson
Mother of Joseph
Born 4/10/62
Died 7/9/74

DULL PLATITUDES AND
BRIGHT IDEAS

To give light to those who sit in darkness and in the shadow of death, to guide our feet into the way of peace.
Luke 1:79 (RSV)

Our son, Rob, was sixteen when he was killed in a freak automobile accident. As word of the sudden tragedy spread, friends and relatives arrived at our home, trying to bring some word of comfort. With the flashing mood changes that I suppose are characteristic of a shock like this, I alternated between being grateful to them for caring enough to come and being angry that they thought anything they could say or do would lessen the terrible pain of our loss.

The ones with whom I had the least patience, who irritated me most, were those who brought religious tracts and books, thrust them into my hands saying, "Read this," and left. Did they actually think my sitting down and reading through those dull platitudes was going to help?

A few nights after the accident, I finally fell into an exhausted sleep. Suddenly I was dreaming of Rob. I saw him, long blonde hair swinging, hurrying along a path that led up a mountain toward a place of brilliant light. He paused to glance back over his shoulder at me, and his smile was brilliant too, his eyes eager. One moment of wordless reassurance - and then he went on, drawn by that beautiful glow. When I awoke, a little of the terrible ache in me had been relieved.

Not long afterward, my husband brought home a book he said he'd found lying in the empty seat of an airliner. The title was LIFE AFTER LIFE. Though I had aimlessly leafed through and then ignored the other books brought to us, I found myself sitting down to read this one. It is a series of accounts by people who have been clinically "dead," telling of the sensations they experienced before they were resuscitated. An overwhelming number described seeing a brilliant light in the distance and receiving the impression that, if they went toward that light, they would know great peace and love.

I had never heard about these "out-of-body" experiences! But after reading that testimony, I am no longer tortured by wondering if those few swift years were all Rob would ever have. He is alive and happy, and I will see him again, I am convinced.

Thank you, Father, not only for helping me to bear my child's death, but for giving me knowledge and courage to face my own.

Martha Orr Conn
Mother of Robert William
Born 6/27/58
Died 2/14/75

13

TAKE COURAGE!

Tears, idle tears, I know not what they mean.
            Alfred, Lord Tennyson

Our son died in June, and in September his sister, Kelley, left for her junior year at The University of Exeter. My husband, Dave, and I joined her in England for Christmas because we were afraid to spend that holiday and New Year's, which would have been Eric's 17th birthday, at home.

A travel writer had suggested that I pay careful attention to billboards and other forms of advertising because they add flavor and authenticity to stories about foreign places. So I found myself reading them all, and recording the ones I liked best.

British life-savers are known as "holes" and their ads for that candy centered on the theme, "Put a hole in your pocket." Rather clever, I thought.

But when I found my favorite, I didn't even realize that it was an advertisement. We were driving into London when I spotted the words "Take Courage" on the side of a building which rose behind the bombed out shell of another. "Oh look," I said, "a remnant from the war. Isn't that just like the British to admonish each other to be brave."

"Mother," my daughter replied with a giggle, "that's the name of an English beer."

We've laughed about that a lot over the years. I misinterpreted those words because I didn't know what was behind them.

After Eric died I tried to "take courage" from the scriptures, but they only made me cry. Now I'm wondering if that happened because I wasn't familiar enough with them at the time, to know what was behind them.

Thank you, Father, for lending me your courage when I couldn't find that strength for myself.

                    Judy Osgood
                Mother of Eric Brett
                  Born 1/1/62
                  Died 6/28/78

THE IMPORTANCE OF FOCUS

When you pass through the waters I will be with you, and when through the rivers, they shall not overwhelm you; when you go through fire you shall not be scorched; or through flames, you shall not be burned. For I am the Lord your God, the Holy One of Israel, your Savior.

Isaiah 43:2-3a (MLB)

My heart ached in knowing sympathy as I read a newspaper story today about a child born with a devastating deformity who died shortly after birth. Her young parents had surely anticipated a perfect little girl; but it was not so. I wondered if they felt angry with God, or abandoned by Him?

The truth is that neither pain, horror, nor broken dreams, though they exist, prove that God does not love us. To the contrary, it was because of these facts, wrought by sin, that God sent Christ. His own agony assures us that nothing can separate us from God's love.

In many respects that mother in the newspaper story is like Mary was in Jerusalem. Nothing then was as Mary would have had it be. She was on a road she hadn't chosen, and I'm sure she felt alone and frightened.

Despair might have won if she had grieved endlessly over the circumstances which had changed her dreams. Instead she turned to that miraculous, lifechanging force within her, and in this she was a model for all of us. When all went wrong, she kept her eyes focused on Him. And He was there.

The greatest battle in life is not with circumstances, but with self.

Lord, help me to believe that you are the answer to pain, and never its cause.

Paula D'Arcy
Mother of Sarah
Born 10/3/73
Died 8/20/75

I AM MADE IN TWO PARTS

There is a right time for everything . . . a time to be born, a time to die; a time to lose; a time to speak up; a time for hating (anger).
Ecclesiastes 3:1, 2, 6, 7, 8 (TLB)

My first real bout with death-related anger emerged an hour after our baby, David, died. In my account of this experience in HIS STUBBORN LOVE, I could not write about that emotion because I felt so guilty. I didn't know that being angry about your loss was normal and that it would pass. I thought Christians were not supposed to have those feelings.

God's love sustained us through the first moments after we learned of the death, but when my husband left the hospital fear and loneliness climbed over the rails of my bed, and when I wasn't looking, anger slipped under the covers with them.

As reality set in, the song of mourning rose to a deafening fortissimo in my ears. My baby was gone. My husband had gone, and I kept wondering why God had chosen this very moment to go, too. I was alone and so angry.

A few years later, C. S. Lewis helped explain that anger for me in his book A GRIEF OBSERVED. He described a woman who had lost her child as being made in two parts. She had a "God-aimed" spirit side and a human motherhood side. He talked of God being a comfort and a hope to her "God-aimed" spirit but not to her mother side. He said, "The specifically maternal happiness must be written off. Never in any place or time will she have her son on her knees, or bathe him, or tell him a story, or plan his future, or see her grandchild."

It seemed an extraordinary miracle of understanding broke inside of me as I read those words. *I am made in two parts.* One responds to God and His touch on my life. I love Him. I trust Him and know He is in control of me and my little world. My baby is well, warm, and is being rocked to sleep in the arms of God. I experience an unexplainable, uncanny peace. I can begin the difficult task of accepting death.

The other part of me? Ah, now that's a different story. The human side, the motherhood side in me - all of this side is not comforted. Am I less a Christian? No! I am just more a mother-human being at this point. My dreams are broken. I can have no more babies. I am angry and wonder over and over, "Why my baby?" "Oh," you say, "but just think - David is with the Lord!" My mother-self rises up and screams out with inescapable anger. "Well, you tell the Lord to give Him back to me. I want him in my arms, not God's." The human side is experiencing the normal reaction of anger.

Anger and the frustrating resentments in and about death are so annihilating few of us can admit it, much less cope with it. But, if we can somehow admit to our anger, either verbally to a close friend or in writing, there comes a degree of healing.

Our Lord understands our anger at death and dying. I suspect when He was hanging on the cross it was the emotion of anger that fired off the words, "My God, my God, why hast thou forsaken me?"

Someday there will be no death or anger. Until then, although there is a time for anger, we must move on, move through it, and move out of its crippling atmosphere. We can do that without guilty regrets because God understands.

Thank you, Father, for helping us to understand ourselves.

Joyce Landorf
Mother of David
Born 12/31/64
Died 12/31/64

I'VE GOT HIM!

I give them eternal life, and they shall never perish, and no one shall snatch them out of my hand.
John 10:28 (RSV)

I bet you thought that if you just loved your child enough and paid very careful attention, nothing could happen - no accident, no illness, no terrible thing could snatch your child away. That's what I thought too.

Did I look away, momentarily distracted by something else? Did I lose my balance or crash into something? I don't think so, but I must have, for in an instant, when I wasn't paying attention, Death came and snatched Matthew, aged almost two, out of my hand.

It happens in other ways. Something breakable slips out of our hand and we give it up for lost, waiting for the crash. Or our favorite pitcher, with two out in the bottom on the ninth and protecting a one-run lead, throws a fat pitch right down the old slot. There's a loud crack, the ball goes sailing, and our heart sinks.

But sometimes, something else happens. Instead of the crash, somebody faster than lightening flicks out a hand and catches whatever it was that we dropped. "It's OK! I've got it!" Or from way out in right field come those faint words, "I've got it!" What relief! What joy!

In that instant of despair, when the surgeon pronounced Matthew dead and everything seemed lost, when my wife and I began to slowly die too, a voice distinct and joyful rang in the ears of our minds - "It's OK! I've got him!"

Ah, we should have known. It's Christ again. Christ of the lightening quick hands, Christ the right-fielder. He caught Matthew at just the right moment. "I give him eternal life," He said. "He shall never perish," He promised. "No one shall ever snatch him out of my hand," He vowed.

I was only me, weak and frail, only human, with no power to prevent Death from snatching Matthew out of my hand. But thank God, thank our great and loving Father in Heaven, that Somebody with fast hands, Somebody who is perfect, Somebody who never misses was there at just the right moment to say, "It's OK! I've got him!"

Thank you, Lord, for having fast hands, and for catching our children when we could no longer hold them.

Dennis Douglass
Father of Matthew
Born 10/22/71
Died 7/27/73

A THOUSAND WHYS

For I know the plans I have for you, says the Lord, plans for welfare and not for evil, to give you a future and a hope . . . You will seek me and find me; when you seek me with all your heart.
Jeremiah 29:11 & 13 (RSV)

After our infant son, Russell, died I searched continuously for answers to the question, "Why?" The first source I turned to for answers was the Bible, and I began by studying passages dealing with affliction, healing and death. As I studied, it became apparent to me that while in some cases the underlying "cause" of the particular affliction was explained, oftentimes it was not.

At the same time I found that some people were miraculously healed, even raised from the dead, but others were not. What made the difference? Why did God appear to respond to some requests while similar requests seemed to fall upon deaf ears? Did He not care? Could He control some events and not others?

My simple "Why?" became many questions, but one thing didn't change. Nothing I read altered my belief in God's absolute sovereignty, or shook my conviction that God doesn't make mistakes.

So where did all of this leave me in my quest for "Why?"

I can't tell you that I found an answer to all my questions. I didn't, but as I read and studied I found that I was gaining a deeper understanding of the character of God. Before I had *known about Him*, but now I feel that I really *know Him* and that has made an enormous difference in my outlook. It has caused the "Whys?" to pale in significance.

I am learning, as the German theologian Dietrich Bonhoeffer suggested, to "find God in what we know, not in what we do not know." That change of direction in my thinking enables me to cope with those unanswered questions. It also leaves me feeling secure in the knowledge that God's plans really are for "my welfare."

Thank you, Father, for helping me to cope with my unanswered questions.

Susan Simon
Mother of Russell
Born 6/5/82
Died 6/5/82

I WILL NOT LEAVE YOU DESOLATE

I will not leave you desolate; I will come to you.
John 14:18 (RSV)

Our youngest child, Becky, was killed in an automobile accident when she was 22. During the first few months following her death I could hardly bear being alone. When I was by myself I often cried uncontrollably and, even though I forced myself to perform necessary household chores, many times I could scarcely see what I was doing for the tears. Fortunately, there were a number of friends who, sensing this, stopped by my house frequently and listened to me talk about her. I know now that this was one way God held me up until I could walk alone.

One such friend, Ann, had known grief first-hand much longer than I. A year before her husband had died of cancer, and eighteen years earlier their four-year-old son had died from leukemia. She brought us a framed copy of the following story.

FOOTPRINTS

One night a man had a dream. He dreamed he was walking along the beach with the Lord. Across the sky flashed scenes from his life. For each scene, he noticed two sets of footprints in the sand; one belonging to him, and the other to the Lord.

When the last scene of his life flashed before him, he looked back at the footprints in the sand. He noticed that many times along the path of his life there was only one set of footprints. He also noticed that it happened at the very lowest and saddest times in his life.

This really bothered him and he questioned the Lord about it. "Lord, you said that once I decided to follow you, you'd walk with me all the way. But I have noticed that during the most troublesome times in my life, there is only one set of footprints. I don't understand why when I needed you most you would leave me."

The Lord replied, "My precious, precious child, I love you and I would never leave you. During your times of trial and suffering, when you see only one set of footprints, it was then that I carried you."

Author Unknown

Ann explained that re-reading this story when she was really hurting had helped her through some rough days. I hung the frame in my bedroom, on the wall beside the dresser, where I could see it each morning. And it has helped me understand how He has helped me through each day - through a friend, a book, a story, a child to love, work to do, people who need me.

Lord, walk with me through this day, and, if I am unable to walk, please carry me.

Peggy Hoyal
Mother of Becky
Born 4/21/59
Died 5/10/81

CHARMI'S LITTLE FLOWER

Then shall the lame man leap like a deer, and the tongue of the dumb shall sing . . .

Isaiah 35:6 (MLB)

My daughter, Charmianne, was sick all the days of her life. When she was 4-1/2 she was released from the hospital to enjoy the last few months at home. A brain tumor had taken 80% of her vision and left both legs paralyzed, so I carried her with me and gave her little jobs to do to keep her busy.

One sunny fall day she wanted to plant flowers so I sat her on the edge of the sidewalk, dug a little hole and handed her a crocus bulb. She put it in the ground carefully and patted the loose soil over it. Then, realizing her hands were dirty, held them out indicating it was time to wash.

Autumn turned to winter, the sun's warmth disappeared, and on a cold and snowy morning in February, Charmi died. I wasn't prepared for her death, even though I knew it was coming, and the days before her funeral were filled with utter despair, mingled with bitterness for the things she was never able to enjoy and for the shortness of her life.

The temperature was so low and the wind so strong the day of her funeral that little balls of ice skipped over the frozen ground. I left for the church not knowing how I could bury my child in that cold earth, and was stopped by a miracle as I stepped outside.

The yellow crocus Charmi had planted had sprung up overnight - leaves, blossom and all. I stared at that sign of God's love and knew that Charmi too was blooming. In my mind's eye I saw her running and jumping in beautiful, flower-filled meadows and I knew that someday, in a place where there is no sickness or death, I'd hold my child in my arms once more. And my heart rejoiced.

Dear Lord, help me to remember that death isn't the end of all joy, but the beginning.

Sandra Hall
Mother of Charmianne
Born 3/10/69
Died 2/6/74

THE DAY THE CLOUDS PARTED

I will lift up my eyes unto the hills, from whence cometh my help.
Psalms 121:1 (KJV)

Before our 16-year-old son, Eric, died of complications stemming from his chemotherapy for bone cancer, he had become an accomplished mountain climber. He always said that he found God in the natural beauty of His Creation.

Since his death five years ago, I have continued to climb and have acknowledged Eric's love of the mountains by signing the summit registers found at the top of major mountain peaks with his name, as well as my own. I usually include a very short explanation that I feel closer to Eric when I am sitting on top of a mountain than at any other time.

Recently, upon arriving at the top of the Middle Teton (in Grand Teton National Park, in Wyoming), on a day in which the peaks were completely swathed in clouds, I became frustrated by the lack of a summit register. After looking for it for several minutes I sat down dejectedly to eat my lunch. .

As I sat there, the clouds parted for a few seconds revealing only the top of the Grand Teton a couple of miles to the North and almost a thousand feet higher. It was as if Eric was saying to me, "It's alright, Dad, you put my name on top of the Grand last year. This one isn't that important."

From that moment on I relaxed and enjoyed my trip back down the mountain, feeling certain that Eric knew I had thought of him.

Father, help us to recognize the signs you give us and to take courage from them.

David Osgood
Father of Eric Brett
Born 1/1/62
Died 6/28/78

ONE CRYSTAL MOMENT

For the first sharp pangs there is no comfort; whatever goodness may surround us, darkness and silence still hangs about our pain.
George Eliot

After our seventeen-year-old son's death, there were moments when I felt as if I were poised above a pit of bottomless despair. During this time, I caught a hint of what the Biblical patriarchs meant when they claimed that they would go down to their graves in sorrow for the loss of their children. Not, as I once thought, that the child's death would precipitate their own, but that, regardless of however long they might subsequently live, they would remember and grieve their lost children. I learned something of the poignancy and depth of sorrow. I reached moments of deep despair.

In one such moment, on the day of his funeral, when I felt that the center could not possibly hold, I silently prayed "Lord, grant me peace and tranquility. I can't find it for myself. It has to come from you." My spirit, a turbulent cauldron of conflicting emotions and thoughts, became a sea suddenly stilled by the Savior. In a world which, for me, had recently gone crazy, I felt a wonderful sense of calm and peace.

Through life, I had been disappointed in a search for definitively answered prayer - Maybe I was getting the answers, but not the ones I anticipated - Yet, here, in one crystal moment of need, where mind and will and spirit hung in the balance, God poured oil upon my troubled waters.

Thank you, Lord, for answering prayer and for your gift of peace, which passes all understanding.

John Paul Curnutt
Father of Cameron
Born 3/8/65
Died 10/9/82

THE PREPARER

The preparations of the heart in man and the answer of the tongue, is from the Lord.
Proverbs 16:1 (KJV)

At a faith workshop for bereaved parents the leader indicated that we limit God by the names we call Him. "Heavenly Father means a loving parent to some people," she said, "but to others the name suggests an authority figure that punishes like a resident policeman." Then together we listed words to describe God that had special meaning for us.

One person said He was the Ultimate Listener. Another suggested He was a Compassionate Friend because He stood by us even when we hurt too much to ask for help.

For me the word that was most meaningful was Preparer. During my child's year-long bout with cancer I became aware of how fully God had prepared us for this terrible experience. Aaron's treatment involved many needles, which were always painful and frightening to him. The nurses decided to teach him hypnosis so that he could get through those procedures with a minimum of discomfort.

During the teaching sessions one of them noticed that at the mere sound of my voice Aaron would "go under" and could endure four tries at an intervenous insertion without flinching. I told her that several years before he and I had developed a bond of communication for visits to the doctor when he had to have shots. I would talk to him and insist he look at me and concentrate on my voice and my touch while I concentrated fully on his face. Our "technique" was as much to help me as to help him.

I had no way of knowing how important that bond would become, but in retrospect I can see that it was a unique way in which God gave us the tools we needed in advance. Our "technique" was a gift to Aaron that never worked with my other child.

Thank you, Lord, for helping us even in ways we fail to recognize.

Lorna Dale
Mother of Aaron
Born 8/24/71
Died 5/19/81

TAKING IT

Without ceasing I mention you always in my prayers.
Romans 1:9 (RSV)

"You're taking it so well!" With sarcastic vehemence my friend, JoAnne, whose daughter was suffering from leukemia, mimicked the sentence we both agreed we were utterly sick of hearing. When my sixteen-year-old son, Rob, was killed in an automobile accident, consoling visitors mistook my shocked numbness for serenity and acceptance. I agreed wholeheartedly with JoAnne, "You show me some way to get out of 'taking it,' and I'll leap at it."

As months went by, I side-stepped "taking it" through avoidance - of friends, neighbors, and relatives. I'd go to my office at odd hours when I knew the building would be empty. I'd shop at stores away from our neighborhood. And after church services (when I went), I became adept at slipping out the side door.

Shutting out those who cared certainly didn't make me any happier. But I kept my tears private, letting them pour out in solitude - while I sorted the family laundry or hid behind a locked bathroom door. Often they'd begin steaming down my face as I drove to my office or to the supermarket.

One day as I sat at a red light, mopping at my damp face with a perennial wad of tissue, I prayed, "Help me, Father, to stop pitying myself. Others have gone through this - why do I feel so alone?" Suddenly I felt a wonderful, loving Force - as if Someone had put His arms around my shoulders.

That day I stopped ducking the people who shared my office building. And that night I opened the door to welcome a neighbor who came bearing gifts - loaves of fresh-baked bread. She looked at me closely. "You're better."

"Yes," I was surprised to hear myself say. "I don't feel so alone anymore."

"We've prayed for that," she said simply.

And then I remembered her note, telling me of the interdenominational group that joined in a prayer chain every morning - at just about the time I had stopped at that red light!

Father, help us to remember that we are never alone.

Martha Orr Conn
Mother of Robert William
Born 6/27/58
Died 2/14/75

THANKS FOR BEING THERE

I will not search the hidden ways
where needs perhaps may hide,
but will instead, the need assuge
that's waiting by my side.

L. M. Voller

When my granddaughter was a patient in a state school, the victim of a rare and fatal illness, I arranged to go there with a tour group in order to visit her while learning more about the school. Our driver was a very nice caring man, and we talked briefly of my personal reasons for going.

We toured the facilities in the charge of a doctor who described each "case." When I knew we were approaching my granddaughter's room I slipped away to see her for a moment alone, to talk to her even though she no longer knew me. I had hoped that somewhere, on some level, my voice might reach and comfort her. Grief and pain crowded in my throat and tears were not far behind.

The rest of the group arrived and the leader began describing the situation concerning this "case." I knew I should have left before they arrived, but somehow I felt my presence was a protection against the impersonal chill of this kind of a tour.

I moved back to make room and was standing there struggling with the ache of unshed tears when I became aware of the emotional support of someone just behind me. There was our driver, not saying a word, but supporting me with his presence. He alone knew that this young girl was much more than just another "case" to me.

Within a short while Laurie died and I kept thinking I would thank this man again, but time gets away and he died too, suddenly. I wrote a letter to his widow and family about it, saying that he would long be remembered by me for his just "being there."

Dear Lord, give us who mourn the early death of our loved ones the ability to comfort others with the comfort wherein we were comforted.

Lucy Voller
Grandmother of Laurie
Born 5/19/70
Died 3/18/72

A CHARMED LIFE

Prayer is not an argument with God to persuade him to move things our way, but an exercise by which we are enabled by his Spirit to move ourselves his way.
                                               Leonard Ravenhill

"What a charmed life I lead!" Someone very dear to me said that impulsively. Then she thought a moment about all the problems she had faced and was still facing, and added, "I must be crazy to say that." I don't think she is because I feel the same way about my life (and hers), and I know why.

My early years were easy in all the ways that count. The first things I remember praying seriously for were admission to the "college of my choice" and the combination of scholarships and student jobs to make it possible.

The next years were a series of prayers for a wonderful husband, his safe return from World War II, the six children and their recoveries from various injuries and illnesses. The Almighty and I had a pretty good thing going; I figured out what I needed, asked for it, He gave (with a few minor modifications), and I said "thank you."

Then at age 31 I began to learn about real life. A hurricane struck southern Connecticut and my parents were drowned in the flood, leaving a young son at home. This had not been in my script, but I figured that, with God's help, all of us would get through it somehow - and we did.

A few years later my sister-in-law took her own life, and we hadn't planned on that either, or the anguish that followed. The guilt over some miraculous thing we should have said or done to ease her despair was a long time going, but, with God's help, it finally did.

The phone call on August 15, 1970, that our 17-year-old son, Tony, had been killed in an auto accident was the real turning point. That was the moment when I turned my life over to God. I thought that I had done so before, but this was different and total. I said, "I am completely helpless. I do not even know what I need. Help me."

And as soon as I said it, I felt a physical sensation of being lifted, as one is lifted by a wave in the ocean. I said yes to everything friends wanted to do for us; they were clearly God's hands here on earth. Not only have we survived, but we have found joy again. Furthermore, we have discovered that we can help others who are grieving.

I still sometimes find myself asking God for something specific, usually for the children or grandchildren, but it doesn't take long for me to remember that they are His at least as much as they are mine, and that His plans for them are undoubtedly better than mine. He would no more wish bad things for them than I would. If they turn to Him, He will help them through whatever happens, as He has always helped me.

Someone once gave me a card with a quotation from St. Francis de Sales on it. It has become the rule of my life, and one I keep passing on to others:

> *Do not look forward to what might happen tomorrow; the same Everlasting Father who cares for you today will take care of you tomorrow and every day. Either He will shield you from suffering, or He will give you unfailing strength to bear it. Be at peace then, and put aside all anxious thoughts and imaginations.*

Thank you, Father, for helping us when we have no idea how to help ourselves.

Ronnie Peterson
Mother of Tony
Born 6/6/53
Died 8/15/70

CHRISTINE'S CHRYSALIS

For this perishable nature must put on the imperishable, and this mortal nature must put on immortality.
I Corinthians 15:53 (RSV)

For years I've known on one level that the butterfly's chrysalis represented the transformation of our souls from the "human" caterpillar, which struggles for existence, to the butterfly, which represents new life in Christ, but when my sister was murdered that symbol took on new meaning for me.

Christine was a gentle, yet exciting person, who took the scripture literally to go the extra mile. She helped Vietnamese refugees in Houston, not only getting them jobs, but also giving them her own belongings, including a new coat off her back. Once a stranger needing a ride in the middle of the night was told, "Go knock on Christine's door, she'll take you wherever you need to go." And Christine did so without a second thought.

Her Christmas cards always depicted the lion lying down with the lamb. Truly my sister was a lamb herself, a woman without enemies who trusted everyone and had no ill feelings for anyone.

"Why then I wondered," as I gazed on her cold, expressionless face "had her life been cut short? Surely God had more work for her to do."

But at the cemetery I understood what was really happening. Butterflies were dancing around the flowers on the casket as it was being lowered into the gravesite, and seeing them I realized that what was being consigned to the earth was merely Christine's chrysalis. Her caterpillar had been transformed and her new life was just beginning.

Thank you, Lord, for the assurance of new life.

Beverly Dornburg
Sister of Christine
Born 1/2/52
Died 8/3/81

SOME NEED A BETTER PLACE

Pray without ceasing.
       I Thessalonians 5:17 (KJV)

In my prayers each morning I had always prayed for each of my children by name - that they might grow in wisdom and strength, and in His grace and truth. I knew surely that this had to be in line with God's will.

But now, Christine, a child of God, murdered? Why? Are the forces of evil stronger than God? How? Where was He? I wondered if I should continue the same prayer for my remaining children.

With mind and heart full of questions, it was only in blind faith that I continued to pray the same prayer for protection and growth for each of our other three children - and an answer came to me one morning:

"Some need a better place to do their growing."

It had been so hard to leave her out of my prayers at first, but now I included her with Thanksgiving in a very special way.

Thank you, Lord, for Your revelations that bring comfort to those of us who mourn.

Hope Blackman
Mother of Christine
Born 1/2/52
Died 8/3/81

LITTLE RAINBOWS

I do set my bow in the cloud, and it shall be for a token of a covenant between me and the earth.
                    Genesis 9:13 (KJV)

As my son and I left the doctor's office, a rainbow looked as though it had gift wrapped the world.

"Look!" Ron exclaimed. "Do you remember how God put the rainbow in the sky as a sign to Noah? Maybe this one is a sign for us."

People have to look for rainbows in life. I believe the little bits of happiness that come into our lives each day are little rainbows from God.

During the last months of his life, Ron became convinced that heaven lay at the end of the rainbow and each rainbow was a promise that God was still aware and concerned with individual problems.

After Ron died, each time we were about to reach bottom in our grief, my husband, daughter and I would see a rainbow - or something symbolic of Ron's philosophy. I'm still overwhelmed when God sends me little rainbows.

February always brings on spells of missing Ron. One Sunday during that difficult month we sang George Matheson's hymn, "O Love That Wilt Not Let Me Go." We didn't sing the third verse, but during the service I glanced down at the open hymnal and these words from it reached up to me in silent benediction:

> *O joy that seekest me through pain,*
>
> *I can not close my heart to thee;*
>
> *I trace the rainbow through the rain,*
>
> *And feel the promise is not vain*
>
> *That morn shall tearless be.*

Dear Lord, thank you for rainbows - even while we're still standing in the rain.

Marie Butler
Mother of Ron
Born 12/26/47
Died 2/17/65

32

I HAD A CHOICE TO MAKE

(God) . . . grant me the serenity to accept the things I cannot change, the courage to change the things I can, and the wisdom to know the difference.

Reinhold Niebuhr

I find that I owe a lot to this prayer, which I discovered years ago when a family member was battling alcoholism. To me it's beautiful because the message it conveys applies to anyone of any faith, or none at all. I needed it then, but nowhere near as much as I need it now.

Sometime ago I gave birth to a beautiful baby girl whom we named Jessica. We brought her home from the hospital believing that she was healthy, but on the 19th day of her life it became clear that something was very wrong. Two days later we were told that she had cancer. There was a malignant tumor in and around her spinal cord.

Jessica died when she was two-and-a-half months old. That fact will never be altered! I could tell. Laundry still needed to be done, dishes piled themselves up in the sink. The dogs still wanted to be let out. My five-year-old son still wanted to hear a bed-time story. That's how I knew that life goes on.

Those signs helped me realize I had a choice to make. I could either continue to stumble around in a dazed-haze, or I could allow myself to change the quality of my survival. If I really wanted to, I could live, love and laugh again as I had done before Jessica died.

I chose to change, and this prayer has made many of my decisions easier. Now when I find myself asking questions about the situation, I also ask, "Can I change this or that?" If not, then I cope by not dwelling as much on the things that I cannot change. What's the sense? They'll still be the same after I worry my heart out! This is important as it gives me more time to deal with the things that I *can* change.

Although it's been two years since Jessica died, this prayer still has a place in my life because it continues to remind me that -

"I alone can make or break my peace of mind."

Anita Carr
Mother of Jessica Renee
Born 12/17/80
Died 2/27/81

LIFE IS A GIFT

The place God calls you to is the place where your deep gladness and the world's deep hunger meet.
Frederick Buechner

On an icy date in late January 1978, I stood beside a bed in the intensive care unit of a Dallas hospital and helplessly watched as our beloved 24-year-old daughter lay in a coma, dying. So many feelings filled my heart. I tried hard to bargain with God: "Please, Father, let me take Julie's place - she's so young - just beginning a beautiful marriage - loving her career as she helps the speechless to speak - serving You in so many ways." But it was not to be; in spite of all the prayers, our beloved died.

On the same date in January 1983, I sat beside the bed of another 24-year-old girl who was dying - Theresa, my Hospice cancer patient. And I thought, as we touched and shared so many feelings, how differently I feel about death five years later. Gone is the fear of death; gone is the fear of inadequacy in the face of death. This time there was no bargaining with God.

As I held her hand she, struggling for each breath, whispered, "I'm not afraid to die. Life is a gift, and now I know I must give it back." And for the moment, we seemed to share the same heartbeat in unconditional love.

The gift I received from working with Theresa and The Compassionate Friends* is the peace that comes through reinvestment, the commitment to your own growth. As we turn to help others, we, in turn are comforted as we grow in faith - the perfect circle.

Thank you, Father, for the healing that takes place in our own hearts when we reach out to others.

> Julie McGee
> Mother of Julie McGee Lamberth
> Born 10/7/53
> Died 1/29/78

* The Compassionate Friends is a self-help group for bereaved parents. For more information write to The Compassionate Friends, P.O.Box 3696, Oak Brook, IL 60522-3696.

THE CONTINUITY OF
NATURE - OF LIFE

The glorious promise of spring, the mystery of summer growth, and the fulfillment of autumn's harvest reveal the greatness and goodness of God.

from THE GATES OF PRAYER

The meaning of this sentence, from the Reform Judaism Prayerbook, has helped me understand and be comforted through a dream about my daughter. It points to the continuity of life.

Mimi, my only child, was 29 years old when she was killed in a car accident. As a clinical psychologist she helped young children with emotional problems. She was a vibrant young woman, devoted to family, friends and the young people with whom she worked. She loved nature, she loved Judaism, she loved life.

In the dream there was a field filled with glorious yellow blossoms. Toward the back I saw Mimi, seated and surrounded by young children, all intent on whatever was transpiring. Then she arose, waved to me, slowly turned and walked away, still in the circle of children.

To me this meant that she is happy and that her influence will always flower in other people's lives. And I believe she was telling me, through the symbol of the continuity in nature, there will be continuity of the love we shared, and that we will be together again. I won't deny that it is a continuous struggle to adjust to her death, that I will miss her always. But whenever I am feeling particularly low, I recall the dream, the tender expression on her face, and I am comforted.

Ruth Eiseman
Mother of Mimi
Born 4/8/49
Died 4/24/78

I THINK I CAN

And indeed everything that was written long ago in the scriptures was meant to teach us something about hope from the examples scripture gives of how people who did not give up were helped by God.
Romans 15:4 (TJB)

Do you remember the story of THE LITTLE ENGINE THAT COULD?

The engine carrying the trainload of toys and good things to eat could not get over the mountain to deliver its contents to the good little boys and girls on the other side.

So (according to the picture in our dog-earred, scribbled-on, well-worn copy), the toy clown flagged down two big engines and asked them for help, but neither could be bothered because they had more important things to do.

The next engine the clown approached had a tired and worn attitude and it chugged away saying, "I can not, I can not, I can not."

Finally, a little blue engine came down the track. She wasn't as big as the other engines and she wasn't very strong, but when the clown asked her for help she hitched herself to the train and chugged over the mountain saying, "I think I can, I think I can, I think I can." And she made it because she believed she could.

Learning to live without my son is the hardest job I've ever had to face. Day after day I've felt like the tired old engine that said, "I can not, I can not, I can not." But sometimes, even on those days, I find myself remembering the little story Eric loved so much when he was small. I remember how he sat on my lap and turned the pages and told me what each engine said. And I remember how, before he got too old for such nonsense, I reminded him of the little blue engine's words when he didn't think he could do something.

And sometimes, when I don't think I can get through the day, I tell myself believing that Eric hears too, "I think I can, I think I can, I think I can" and knowing he believes in me as I believed in him, I make it through.

Thank you, Father, for happy memories that help us live without the children we love.

Judy Osgood
Mother of Eric Brett
Born 1/1/62
Died 6/28/78

OUT OF A DARK AND PAINFUL STRUGGLE

Where were you when I laid the foundation of the earth?
Job 38:4 (RSV)

My son took his own life shortly after his 18th birthday. To me it was a life interrupted - a life that did not have a chance for fulfillment. I could not understand why he chose death instead of life. Was love the reason? We had always been close. I loved him in a special way and knew that he loved me. So why . . .?

Suicide, to me, is the ultimate form of rejection and I really had to wrestle with that, yet as I did so I realized that for him it was the only way out of a pain so great that for him there was no other answer . . . and I, loving him, could not wish him here with me only to satisfy my own need to love and to be loved.

In my own dark struggle to find some answers I wrote this poem on the second anniversary of his death. Through this wrestling-writing process I found some meaning in his death and eased my pain when I let go of some of the questions.

> *Do not ask why of God . . . He knows but will not*
> *share.*
> *He feels the pain with me and cares, and that should*
> *be enough.*
> *He does not ask that I control the universe with Him,*
> *But that I live each day in love and trust that He is*
> *holding him.*
> *And as the years go by and tears no longer flow,*
> *I realize that with the pain, God's given me the chance*
> *to grow.*

Lord, thank you for the gift of life.

Pat Hummel
Mother of Don
Born 2/28/56
Died 4/29/74

JUST FOR A MINUTE, GOD

In the day when I cried thou answeredst me, and strengthenedst me with strength in my soul.

Psalms 138:3 (KJV)

Life seemed to end for me when my son, Tim, died. That wasn't the way it was supposed to happen! I believed that life was eternal and death was only a door, but I held those beliefs for myself, not for my children.

Doubts crept into my mind in spite of my efforts to keep them at bay. Did that hateful wound in the earth really hold only the body of my son while his spirit and soul survived, or was "eternity" a myth to help us accept reality?

Repeatedly I begged God to let me see him just for a minute so I would know he was all right.

I rarely take naps, but one day I was so overcome with drowsiness that I gave in to the impulse to sleep and dropped exhausted onto my bed. Sleep came almost instantly, yet at the same time I seemed to be totally awake. And he was there!

Tim stood before me as clear and as real as he had been in life. He didn't speak, but in my mind I heard his voice say, "O.K., Mom. You wanted a minute so you've got a minute. So look at me. See, I'm fine." His tone was teasing, but he sounded a bit put out at my worry.

"It can't be Tim," I thought, "he's dead!" When I finally accepted him as real, I tried to take in every detail. His lean, craggy face held an expression I had never seen on this earth and will never see again, I'm sure. For that face held absolute peace and absolute beauty. He did not speak again but only stood smiling that slightly crooked smile I remembered so well, and in a few more seconds he was gone.

I was awake now, and with my sleep had gone my doubts of Tim's survival. God had granted me my minute with Tim. Was it only a dream? Perhaps. But if it was, it was the sweetest dream of my life because it gave back my faltering faith in double measure.

Lord help me to accept the minutes and use them to the fullest for they are what eternity is made of.

Judy Dickey
Mother of Tim Hughes
Born 8/31/54
Died 7/20/79

LOVE TO SHARE

A broken and contrite heart, O God, you will not despise.
Psalms 51:17 (NIV)

It was so hard to face each day after my son died. Matt, who was 17-1/2, was killed in an automobile accident the day after he graduated from high school.

He was all that a young man should be; all that I had ever wanted in a son - a loving, giving boy with the promise of the future in his grasp.

The days were crushing without that boy to share life's song, but, despite the intensity of despair the bond of love between us kept me afloat. I felt it each spring as I saw the birds we both enjoyed return to our backyard, as the flowers that he chided me about bloomed again, and as the skies filled with the snow that he loved.

As the seasons came and went I began to feel in my heart it was God's way of saying to me, "See, things have not changed. Nothing can take away the love that you shared and still feel between you. Share it with others; it is yours to give."

When Matt had been dead five years I learned about The Compassionate Friends and three years later I took over as our chapter's leader. At one meeting another mother who had lost her son said, "All I want is to still be his Mother."

Her words echoed in my heart and in my head. That was the unspoken cry of every bereaved mother. It was what I wanted too, and it is the gift that God has given me.

No, my son hasn't been miraculously brought back to life. Instead I've discovered that he lives through me as I put my love for him to work helping others. Doing that has brought me so much joy and satisfaction that finding new ways to share that love has become my goal for the rest of my life's journey.

Oh God, help me to feel always the peace of mind and heart that I know now.

Dorothy Pisapia
Mother of Matthew
Born 9/30/55
Died 6/10/73

LOVE'S ROAD

I shall be telling this with a sigh
Somewhere ages and ages hence:
Two roads diverged in a wood, and I -
I took the one less traveled by,
And that has made all the difference.

Robert Frost
from THE ROAD NOT TAKEN

During the first months after the death of my husband and child I locked myself inside my apartment. When the phone rang I stared at the receiver until it was still. Friends knocked at my door, calling my name, and I wouldn't answer. If my arms could not hold the ones for whom I longed, then I wanted them empty. My angry choice.

And my private choice, too. For I was building hard barriers inside of me. In subtle, secret ways I had begun to say "No" to all of life because part of life had hurt me.

Then one day, unexpectedly, my mail contained a letter from a young man in Kansas. He was suffering from a painful and incurable illness and he wanted my friendship. To my chagrin he would not accept any of my "public" faces, nor would he honor my walls. He hammered into my life demanding that I be there. Without regard he pushed past the shadows and the memory-filled half person I was willing to become. His insistence was like a scream that I be alive.

In effect he was forcing me into the yellow wood and demanding that I face its reality: one inviting road of memories and shadows; and the other, rough road of love. No one grieves without standing at that same fork, waiting to decide. For it's never that we can't love again. It's that we won't. I knew. I had refused for a long, long while.

The experience of this encounter was the beginning of my fearful steps toward all the possibilties which might be waiting in my new, altered life. It was when I began to live for the new day. It was when I agreed to say goodbye to what had been. It was when I first started re-accepting life. Life in general, and my life in particular.

During those hard weeks when my choices were made I assumed that their significance reached only to my future. Today I see that I was very mistaken. For how we choose to survive casts as much light (or darkness) on our treasured past as it does on our anticipated future. Here is the key: Nothing can give lasting life to the loves of yesterday except our willingness to carry the experience of that love onto the new roads sent for us to travel. In denying the new we bury the old. For when we cling to memory and live only with regret we do not really have that which we so tightly grasp.

Nothing is ours until we let it go. That's the mystery of life and death both.

Lord, give each one who reads these words the courage to take love's road.

Paula D'Arcy
Mother of Sarah
Born 10/3/73
Died 8/20/75

A BEWILDERING EXPERIENCE

He will guide them to springs of living water; and God will wipe away the tears from their eyes.
Revelations 7:17b (RSV)

It must have been a bewildering experience, to be called out of whatever went before and into incarnation at the union of a sperm cell and an egg. I wonder if he missed wherever it was he came from?

And then, nine months later, he was expelled from the womb into a new world of harsh lights and sounds, a world of hunger and pain and confusion. I wonder if he remembered the womb? I wonder if perhaps his birth cries might not have been cries of loss at being parted from the familiar and thrust into the unfamiliar?

And twenty-one months later, it happened again. There was the hospital, but he had known hospitals. And there was the gurney, but he didn't know gurneys. His last drowsy shout as they wheeled him away toward surgery was, "Mom!"

And then he went to sleep, and when he woke up, he was someplace else again, someplace he'd never been before. Not a hospital, not an earthly home. Someplace else.

Did he cry? Did he feel a sense of loss leaving his earthly family? Was he confused or afraid?

But the Shepherd was there, waiting for him. The Shepherd healed the horrible wound of his operation and led him to a spring where he could quench his thirst.

And then a wonderful thing happened. His new Heavenly Father reached down and picked him up. He gently held the little boy and said, "There, there, Matthew, no need to cry anymore." And He reached up and wiped the tears from Matthew's eyes.

Yes, I'm sure that's how it happened, and how, someday, it will happen for each of us. He will guide us to springs of living water, and God will wipe away the tears from our eyes.

Dear Father, thank you for wiping the tears from our eyes now, and for loving and caring for our children.

Dennis Douglass
Father of Matthew
Born 10/22/71
Died 7/27/73

LET ME GO!

THE ANSWER

When for a purpose I had prayed and prayed and prayed
Until my words seemed worn and bare with arduous use,
And I had knocked and asked and knocked and asked again,
And all my fervor and persistence brought no hope,
I paused to give my weary brain a rest
And ceased my anxious human cry.
In that still moment, after self had tried and failed,
There came a glorious vision of God's power,
And, lo, my prayer was answered in that hour.

Lowell Fillmore

In 1979, on the fourth anniversary of her transition, I was celebrating the life of my beautiful, creative, artistic, 24-year-old daughter, Viki (an accidental cocaine suicide), by preparing for the first meeting of The Compassionate Friends chapter in Palm Desert, California, when I had an experience I'd like to share.

While typing a poem, I was overcome by the profound grief I had worked so diligently to resolve. I got still and simply let go. Instantly, my sobs were quieted by the awareness of the presence of Viki's consciousness. Crystal clearly, her voice came to my inner hearing, saying, "Hey, Mom, that's enough with the grief, a'ready. Release me." I did, lovingly and gratefully.

In that moment, I realized that after three years of grief therapy, Bible study and all my human prayers, my resolution had not included release. My continued grieving was holding Viki back from her on-going higher good. By releasing her, I am truly healed of my mortal grief, and the Spirit of Viki is free for expression in that other dimension of existence beyond human understanding.

Thank you, Father-Mother God, that this is so.

Jean D. McIntyre
Mother of Viki
Born 7/26/50
Died 9/5/75

WHEN GRIEVING IS POSTPONED

Defenses erected against suffering will stifle our lives and leave us with another kind of suffering, more painful than that which we sought to evade.

Elizabeth O'Connor

"You just had a little girl that looks perfectly okay . . . but she's dead. We don't understand why and would like your permission to do an autopsy."

The euphoria of delivery vanished.

A nurse, holding a blurry bundle with a newborn face asked, "Do you want to hold her?"

A few hot tears ran down my cheeks as I shook my head "no," controlling my feelings as I always had.

There was an enormous lump in my stomach - a wound deep inside. I began rationalizing to relieve the pain.

"Just think of all the dirty diapers I won't have to change," I told myself. In that moment, small relief appeared, only to vanish when the judge in me screamed, "How can you think that!" Renewed awareness of the loss came rushing back.

Whenever feelings of disappointment, anger or guilt arose, I prayed to be rid of them, focusing instead on persons for whose care I was thankful. Knowing they cared was balm, unexpected and over-whelming.

There were some who added to the hurt like the student nurse who asked, "What do you have to cry about?" And the well-intentioned, "It must be God's will," which only supported my feeling that God was punishing me for my failure as a mother to my other two children.

My family put the bassinet and baby chest away and we entered into an unspoken agreement to protect each other (and ourselves) by not talking about "it."

The grief did not disappear; it sank into deep recesses. My grieving was postponed.

It erupted unannounced some years later in the midst of a death and dying workshop. And again after the death of one of my little son's friends. Again and again. Each time I plummeted closer to the depth of my anguish. And each time, more healing of that deep wound took place.

I know now that I handled my grief the way I needed to at the time. But, the more I let myself feel and express, the more I healed. The more painful feelings I expressed, the more I was able to feel feelings of all kinds! I not only healed, but grew more whole as a person.

Our Creator made us creatures of feeling. Jesus, too, wept. And when we choose to let ourselves experience the sufferings by feeling the pain, we become more at-one within ourselves and within the human race.

Lord, we lean on You knowing that because You have suffered too, no amount of pain can separate us from Your love.

Barbara Somerville Rice
Mother of Laura Beth
Stillborn 10/21/69

SEND ME A ROSE

Lord, I believe; help thou mine unbelief.
Mark 9:24 (KJV)

On April 16, 1977 the deputy sheriff of Upson County, Georgia, called with the brutal news that both our son and daughter had been killed in a fiery plane crash. "Why our beautiful children?" we asked as we struggled to retain our sanity. "Why us?"

Ruth's Story

My faith was so important to me and so much a part of my life that I had never known it to waver before, but in the depths of my grief it didn't keep me from needing assurance that my children were with God. "Send me a rose, Lord," I begged. "Then I will know my sweet babes are in Your arms." I didn't know what to expect, or even if God would answer me, but I had to ask.

A few hours later we went shopping and when we came back a friend's car was in our driveway. As we pulled up behind it she got out and handed me twelve long-stemmed red roses. I realized, instantly, that God had answered my prayer, and I looked toward the heavens and cried. Somehow . . . someway . . . He had heard my plea for aid.

That was all I needed, but it wasn't all that He had to give. Early the next morning a dear friend stopped in to see me and handed me one long-stemmed red rose. Taking it from her I held it to my lips in awe, and as I did so a close relative came in and thrust another rose just like it into my hand. Both explained that they were mysteriously compelled to "take a rose to Ruthie." No logic could account for this happening except that it was our Lord's way of saying, "My child, I have heard you. They are here with Me."

46

George's Story

Shortly after we lost our children I was walking along the seashore trying to quell the stinging anger that boiled within me, but despite my efforts those pent-up emotions burst forth in a tirade of uncontrolled bitterness towards God. I walked out into the surf up to my knees and over the crashing waves called to Him for answers and comfort. Nothing happened. Finally, I challenged Him to send me one of the elusive sand dollar shells that rarely come this close to shore, if our children were with Him.

Magically, a tiny, perfect white sand dollar floated into my outstretched hand. Looking up into space I felt a wave of tranquil peace sweeping over me and knew that He had answered. I thanked Him, although a shade of doubt lay hidden in my mind. But then I felt something brushing against my leg and, looking down, I saw a second sand dollar nestled against me. Indeed, our generous Lord was making sure that I had heard Him.

Thank you, dear Lord, for talking to us through your creations.

.

George & Ruth Nutting
Parents of
George Leonard, Jr.
Born 12/9/50
Died 4/16/77
and
Doris Ruth
Born 6/28/54
Died 4/16/77

I DIDN'T WANT TO DO IT!

Do when you don't want to do. Go when you don't want to go. . . .
and when you least expect it, you may glimpse the open door to
Revelation.

Nina Herrmann

Ten years ago I was a happy, fulfilled mother and wife, but our family's "successful" life came to an abrupt end when our beautiful and precious son, Rhys, aged eleven, was killed in an auto accident. Suddenly we were a traumatized family - mother, father and two teenage daughters, struggling to keep on going, but emotionally devastated.

In my rage I cried, "Where are you, God? Why did you do this to me? To us? Why did you take Rhys? I know he won't be happy with you . . . he liked it here with us! When is all this pain going to end? Can't you hear me?"

Time passed. As my husband, Lindsay, went through the agonies of (misplaced) guilt and depression, his business suffered and he lost interest in it. With no outlet or counselling for the enormous trauma he had suffered, he became angry and very difficult to live with.

Our beach house was the only place where I could let off steam, cry, think, pray and just be myself. Some days I washed the beach with my tears. Other times I found peace and comfort as I watched the waves.

Two years went by, though I can't remember very much about them. However, without realizing what was happening, two "answers" to my prayers came into my life in the form of two new friends. The first was a nun - a warm, caring, and beautiful Irish sister. She and others from her order visited us, loved us, listened to us, boosted us up, and never preached to us.

A year later, God sent the second messenger, a sensitive friend - more earthy and materialistic than the nun, but one who was very empathetic and deeply involved in telephone counselling. She encouraged me to join this service, which I did, and for the first time, my thoughts were switched from my own misery to the feelings and needs of others.

Later Lindsay joined me in this endeavor and together we discovered that our personal sorrow deepened our awareness of other people's feelings. Our shared enthusiasm meant that we had a vital interest together, and we began to heal and grow.

Then, much later, through our work, came the awareness of the complete lack of any supportive, caring services for bereaved parents

48

in Australia, which we ourselves had experienced when we had most needed it. One night we read an article about The Compassionate Friends, which we had never heard of. We both said . . . "If only we had that here. We need it so much!" Then God spoke to us firmly by simultaneously planting an idea in both our minds. There could have been no doubt of His intention. . . . We suddenly looked at each other and knew we were the ones to start it.

I can truthfully say at that time, I didn't want to do it. I fought against it. I had a sickening feeling in my stomach. I was starting to get better. I didn't want to get back into grief again. I wanted a new lifestyle; to have fun again; to enjoy my daughters and their activities. But it didn't happen that way. The very next morning found me traveling into the city of Melbourne to speak to a journalist at our leading newspaper to ask for publicity for our new venture.

There can be no doubt in my mind now that He intended us to do this work. Right from the start it was as if we had plugged into a force of untapped need. The Compassionate Friends took off with an enthusiasm which often left me far behind. I didn't always find it easy or fulfilling.

Lindsay, however, was my best friend. He worked steadily alongside me with great dedication. He sustained me and built up a strength and wholeness which made me love him more than ever, in a totally new way. Through the strangest and saddest lifestyle, we became absorbed in and committed to each other once again.

Now The Compassionate Friends in Australia is firmly established. It is a proven reality, utilizing the resources of our State Government of Victoria in the establishment of the world's first Bereaved Parent Drop-In Support and Information Centre.

My life has been enriched beyond measure with beautiful friends and a worthwhile job to do . . . yet, for so long I fought against all that has happened to me and berated God in prayer, feeling that I knew so much better than He did, what was best for me. I don't know what the years ahead will bring, but I know that I still have many roads to travel and truths to discover and that He'll be with me all the way.

Lord, for the rest of my life, give me the grace of acceptance and build up my strength to cope with whatever may happen to me.

Margaret Harmer
Mother of Rhys
Born 6/8/62
Died 10/28/73

THE "NEW" OLD WALNUT TREE

I will not leave you comfortless, I will come to you.
John 14:18 (KJV)

A small walnut tree appeared in our garden one spring. It probably came from a nut hidden by a squirrel. Martin, my husband, pulled it and tossed it in the trash.

Another tree appeared. I pulled it. This scene was repeated several times before we discovered our pre-schoolers, Ron and Kathy, were replanting it.

We let it grow. It eventually provided shade for the yard and a feast of walnuts for the neighborhood.

When Ron was 16, we learned he had cancer. In spite of crutches, he helped gather the fall crop of walnuts. He chuckled and said, "Only God can make a tree, but Kathy and I helped it survive." I think Ron knew he was gathering his last crop.

We moved several times after Ron's death. One day, I drove by our former home. Someone had cut the walnut tree. That vacant spot reinforced my feelings that life offered me nothing but endings.

Several months later, Martin came to the kitchen window and said, "I want you to see something in the flower bed."

There was a tiny walnut tree about the size of the one we tried to throw away long ago.

"It's strange," Martin said. "That's where I dumped dirt from our porch boxes right after we moved here. That nut probably came from . . ."

Words were not necessary. We were each lost in fond memories. What could be more symbolic of God's love and compassion than a seedling from our children's tree?

Our "new" tree stands by the drive, a reminder that life also offers new beginnings.

Thank you, Lord, for symbols of your love that appear quite unexpectedly.

Marie Butler
Mother of Ron
Born 12/26/47
Died 2/17/65

THE HARDEST PERSON TO FORGIVE

Dynamic psychology (teaches) that we can achieve inner health only through forgiveness - the forgiveness not only of others but also of ourselves.

Joshua Loth Liebman

When a good friend's husband died some years ago, I turned to the literature on grief searching for advice on how to help her. Among other things, I read about grief-related guilt and was really struck by the fact that parents who have lost a child to cancer always seem to find something to feel guilty about because they couldn't prevent their child's death. In essence the book said that if they couldn't find anything, they'd make something up.

I remembered that when my son's cancer was diagnosed, and knowing my own tendency to try and absorb the guilt of the world, I resolved not to let that happen to me. From the very beginning I told myself that I would take such good care of him that even if he died, and, of course, I didn't expect him to, I'd be able to look back and say, "It wasn't my fault. I did everything I could." I would not allow myself to be overwhelmed with regrets.

But it didn't work. Eric died, and when he did I was consumed with guilt as well as grief. Each morning I woke up crying and as I forced myself to get up, looked at our son's picture on the wall and begged him to forgive me for letting him die. The months passed and that ritual continued because I couldn't forgive myself. Nor did I realize I needed to.

I cannot point to a magical moment when I was filled with relief because I forgave myself. The truth is, I didn't even realize I'd done that until I was reading Keith Miller's book, THE TASTE OF NEW WINE. In it he says, "I found that although I had believed God could forgive me for all my selfishness and sins, I discovered that I could not forgive myself for one of them in particular."

I saw myself in that experience and realized, in retrospect, that I had moved beyond my guilt when I accepted the fact I did the best I could, and forgave myself because that wasn't enough to save my child's life.

Help us to forgive ourselves, Father, as you taught us to forgive others.

Judy Osgood
Mother of Eric Brett
Born 1/1/ 62
Died 6/28/78

51

WHAT GOOD CAN COME OF THIS?

All things work together for good to them that love God.
Romans 8:28 (KJV)

A few months after my son's death, I went, with many misgivings, to a writer's conference for which I had signed up prior to the accident. Near the end of the week, I confided the reason for my depression to another conferee, an elderly woman. She began, "Oh, my dear, I lost a child when he was four, and it's very hard. But you do get over it; you learn to . . ."

She couldn't go on. The tears had begun to roll down her cheeks, and her eyes betrayed the undying pain of that long-ago bereavement. In despair, I thought, "You never get over it."

Eight years later, I realize that is true - and not true. You do get past it - and you do learn and grow (slowly and rebelliously, perhaps), until a verse like Romans 8:28 no longer makes you want to throw down the Bible and scream, "What possible good came of my child's death?"

It has taken me a long time, but after fighting my way through all the anger, depression, despair, and remorse, I have been able to find in our loss these "good" results:

1. An enduring marriage. In the first months after Rob died, I thought our marriage might have been destroyed too. For the first time, when I was hurting and needing comfort badly, the person I'd always counted on to "be there" for me couldn't be. My husband was hurting too badly himself. And when, occasionally, I looked beyond my own misery, I wasn't able to think of much to say or do to relieve the agony on his face.

Gradually, we learned simply to endure together, until time began the healing. (It does - ever so slowly - but it does.)

2. A closer family. We have learned the hard way not to take our loved ones for granted. Many times we've thought, "Why didn't we just sit and talk with Rob more?" "Why didn't we show him more affection, give him more praise?" "Why didn't we go places and do things together more often?"

The only way to ease these regrets is to show our appreciation of the family that is left to us. We are much more openly affectionate now, and we remember to say, "I love you" often.

3. A deeper gratitude for my church and surer faith in its teachings. For me, church attendance had been a habit, something I'd been taught to

do on Sundays. I had never known there could be such comfort and strength in the real love and concern of my fellow believers.

Their prayers, their caring, helped us in so many ways. Particularly, their loving-kindness did much to dim my husband's cynical memories of the uncharitable and intolerant church he had experienced in boyhood.

Before Rob died, I hoped there was something beyond this life. Now I am sure there is. This convinction came as a last gift from our son, and I treasure my certainty that I will someday join him in a world of peace and love.

Am I being a Pollyanna? I don't think so. Though God cannot always protect us from times of terrible struggle and loss, He does always offer His bounteous love to help us through. Nor does He hold against us those first bitter days when we cry and curse Him for what has happened. He probably cries with us.

Father, thank you for helping us to endure. Comfort us, forgive us our times of bitterness and despair, and lead us to acceptance.

Martha Orr Conn
Mother of Robert William
Born 6/27/58
Died 2/14/75

MY SOURCE OF STRENGTH

God is our refuge and strength, a very present help in trouble.
Psalms 46:1 (KJV)

God has been a part of my life for as long as I can remember, but I have never felt the presence of a being so powerful and loving as I did a few hours after my son, Max, died.

My 18-year-old daughter was home alone when the police came to tell us about the accident. I was 300 miles away. On the way back I wondered, with every turn of the wheels, how I would respond when I reached my destination. When my baby died twenty years before I had gone into the house, drawn the draperies and not come out again for 18 months. Only then because I realized my little son was growing without sunshine and little boys need sunshine. Only then for this boy who now too was dead.

And so it was with the fear of my own response that I opened the door to the apartment. My daughter was weeping pitifully and crying my name, but I did not fall apart. I did not run away this time, as I had before, because I was lifted up with so much strength that I was filled with power.

Well meaning friends had stripped the living room of all signs of Max. His guitar was put away and his picture taken from the wall. As soon as I had comforted my daughter and hugged my friends I brought both of them out again, and told everyone that we had to face what had happened. We could sit before his picture and weep, but we had to face it. I knew from experience that I could not have functioned that well alone, but the strength of that powerful, loving Presence enabled me to begin my grief work then and there.

Thank you, Father, for being there so that I may say, "Whence cometh my strength? My strength cometh from the Lord."

Fay H. Harden
Mother of Max Raymond Smith
Born 7/17/56
Died 4/14/78

THE TRUTH MARK RELIED ON

And all things whatsoever ye shall ask in prayer, believing, ye shall receive.

Matthew 21:22 (KJV)

The small red New Testament that had been issued to each Marine recruit was crisp and new, but the words were familiar to our 18-year-old son, Mark. He flipped through the pages until he found a favorite verse, underlined it and shared it with his girlfriend as we waited for him to board his flight to bootcamp.

That was the start of a whole new chapter in his life, and a happy time for Mark. For years he had dreamed of becoming a marine. During his basic training he began to really rely on the promises he had learned God could fill, if he would just ask. And he openly praised and thanked God for the blessings he received. In one of his letters he said, "We know who allowed me to be the best in the platoon, don't we Mom!"

About a year later two marine officers stood at attention in our living room and told me that Mark had been killed in an auto accident. That day began a new chapter in my life, which I have come to think of as "the first day of the rest of my life."

Six years have passed since then and in that time I've discovered and rediscovered and re-rediscovered the truth Mark relied on at boot camp, that God helps us when we ask. Often the assistance hasn't come as fast as I had hoped, and sometimes the answer isn't what I expected, but always in this healing process God has helped me take the steps that I couldn't take alone.

Thank you, Father, for Mark's example that has helped me cope with his death.

Joyce Gabriel
Mother of Mark Earl
Born 5/15/57
Died 2/12/77

SCRAMBLED, PLEASE

If you can't change circumstances, change the way you respond to them.

Tim Hansel

In the weeks and months immediately following my son's death I told God over and over the things I thought He needed to know about the care and feeding of my teenaged boy. "Eric likes his steaks rare," I said, "and he prefers scrambled eggs for breakfast with at least five pieces of bacon on the side. More if he can talk me out of it."

I knew my son was in heaven and I also knew that he was old enough to take care of himself, but I couldn't stop praying for him as though he were still alive. At the same time I felt uneasy doing so, as if my prayers implied I no longer trusted God. To compensate I apologized every day, after I told Him what I thought He needed to know. Still, my guilty feelings grew.

Then one day, about six months after Eric died, I received a note from my friend, Joan, who is also a bereaved parent. Her Kenny was 17 when he lost his battle with muscular dystrophy. "I used to beg God to take care of my son," she said. "Now instead I say, 'Thank you, God, for taking such good care of him.'"

Instinctively I knew that what she was doing was important, and I decided to give it a try. "Thank you, God," I said, somewhat tentatively, "for taking such good care of Eric."

No, it didn't ease my mind immediately. In fact, it took weeks before I meant what I said. But gradually I got to the point where I could see that those prayers were part of my inability to give up my mothering role. They weren't an expression of hidden doubts. They were just another step in letting go, a perfectly normal step for a grieving parent. And when I realized that, the guilt feelings disappeared.

Thank you, Father, for continuing to love me when I try to tell you how to do your job.

Judy Osgood
Mother of Eric Brett
Born 1/1/62
Died 6/28/78

56

SOMETIMES GOD SPEAKS
THROUGH SYMBOLS

Jesus answered, "Everyone who drinks this water will be thristy again, but whoever drinks the water I give him will never thirst. Indeed, the water I give him will become in him a spring of water welling up to eternal life."

John 4:13-14 (NIV)

A short time after our son, Matt, died following open heart surgery, we went hiking in the mountains. Our objective was a mountain crater. It was a hot, dusty day in late summer and the climbing was hard work.

As we walked, we passed cold springs and streams, and icy, tumbling water from the glacier. How the water sparkled and danced in the sun! My mouth was dry, my throat was parched, but thirsty as I was, I couldn't stoop and drink. My throat tightened as I remembered Matt's thirst before surgery. The doctors had warned us that the anesthetic would flush out his tissues, but that he shouldn't have a drink. It seemed a small matter at the time. But as we continued climbing, Matt's thirst loomed large. Foolishly, I felt that because I couldn't meet his last little human need then, I had to deny my own need now.

But God is good. He often comes to us when we are foolish and vulnerable. And that day, along that mountain path, God nudged my memory and opened my clenched heart. He brought me the words of John 4:13-14, reminding me that this water that danced so merrily alongside the trail, while as fleeting as Matt's brief life, symbolized the living water of Christ, the true water from which Matt had already drunk and quenched an eternal thirst.

A symbol. I bent over and filled my cupped hands with the water, thankful for this communion with Matt and with all those I love in the Spirit.

Father, thank you for the Living Water that quenches our spiritual thirst and unites us with those we love.

Ruth Douglass
Mother of Matthew
Born 10/22/71
Died 7/27/73

THE KEY IS LOVE

His banner over me was love.
Song of Solomon 2:4 (KJV)

Why, when I know you are not there, am I drawn to the place where your body lies?

Why am I filled with such peace and strength while I tend your own small piece of real estate - to clip the grass around the monument we made for you - to take away the weathered flowers and replace them with new ones - to house-keep for you in a motherly fashion, the only way I can now.

Why is my muddled mind seemingly soothed and smoothed as if the hand of God had personally, gently wiped away the creases and wrinkles that were causing distress, leaving me in peace temporarily. Can it be because this is the last physical place you'll ever occupy? Or is it that I know I love my God even more now that I have surrendered you solely to his care?

It seems the key to it all is love - the legacy of love you left us and the love God showered on us when He gave His Son's life for yours.

Thank you, Father, for enabling me to find beauty even when the path is dark.

                    Fay H. Harden
                    Mother of Max Raymond Smith
                    Born 7/17/56
                    Died 4/14/78

THE ROYAL-BLUE BUTTERFLY

How great are his signs, how mighty his wonders!
Daniel 4:3 (NIV)

During the year my son Aaron was ill from cancer, we talked several times about his death. He was bothered by the fact he didn't know anyone in heaven. One day I showed him pictures of my grandparents and told him stories about them, thinking that would help. It didn't. "It's not the same as knowing them," he said.

Another time, certain that I knew what would reassure him, I announced with enthusiasm. "I know the answer, Aaron. You know Jesus." Thoughtfully he looked at me then slowly said, "Yes, Mommy, I do, but I don't know what He looks like."

My inability to ease Aaron's concern continued to trouble me.

Then one day, near the beginning of winter, Aaron met Shannon at a hospital party. Though they were unlikely friends, he was 9 and she was 14, a strong bond formed between them. The only thing they had in common, which they never discussed, was the fact that they were both likely to die from their illnesses.

And one early morning in May, Shannon did. That evening, as I was settling into bed at home, I "saw" her. I don't know if it was a dream, though it didn't have the same quality as one, but I do know that it wasn't a conscious fantasy. She was wearing a white dress and standing on a green hill. The sun was shining and a breeze was gently blowing her long hair. I was aware of the fact that she wasn't in heaven. It was behind her, out of my sight, but near. Shannon held her hands out and up, cupped gently, waiting. A few inches above her hands hovered a giant, royal-blue butterfly. My first conscious thought later was, "Butterflies aren't royal blue."

Two days later I attended her funeral and six days after that said a last goodby to my Aaron dressed for his funeral, as we had always planned, in his royal-blue cub scout uniform.

The butterfly had come to rest in Shannon's hands.

Thank you, Father, for friendships that sustain us in this world and last into the next.

Lorna Dale
Mother of Aaron
Born 8/24/71
Died 5/19/81

A MESSAGE FROM TEDDY

*The value of life is not measured by one's longevity, but by the
quality of one's love. Life is transient. Love is not.*
                                                    Paula D'Arcy

When he wasn't talking, he was writing. From the day he mastered
the alphabet, Teddy wrote constantly - stories, letters, diaries, plans -
there seemed to be no bounds to his interests and imagination.
His account of our move from Denver to Maryland was both descriptive
and amusing - the sights along the way, the friends we stayed with,
interactions with his brothers and sister and "Baby Dog" - and in a
tender, moving line he described waking his mother on one of those
mornings, seeing "the sunrise that was in her eyes." That was a true
measure of how he adored her.

His father - now that was a different matter. In one hilarious page of
short essays typed for school, he described how fathers never answer
your questions, they just launch off into long speeches about how it
was when they were young. He knew how to keep me humble.

Teddy persisted with his writing even after a cranial hemorrhage and
critical surgery at age 11. During the long months of recovery, when
his handwriting was shaky, he discovered the typewriter. Pecking
away, he continued to record his thoughts and hopes and dreams. All
through his early teens he put his soul into print.

During the summer of 1979 I noticed him typing away furiously,
surrounded by address books and telephone directories. I kept asking
if I could help, and he finally said, in desperation, "Oh, Dad, you're
going to spoil everything!" So I backed off. I knew a project brewing
when I saw one.

Then one terrible day in August of that year, a second hemorrhage left
him paralyzed. He lived six weeks beyond that date and sometime
during that interval we discovered, from a letter returned because of a
wrong address, that his project was soliciting memories of the Tiede-
manns from friends for a Quarter Century Album for our 25th wedding
anniversary. His brother and sister finished the project for him after
his death, and it is one of the most precious treasures that he left us.

Teddy's written legacy keeps alive the memory of his wit, his sensitivity
and, above all, his love for us. My favorite of his writings is a poem
which he called "Decisions." The last four lines of it read:

As my dark thoughts clear,
My soul gains its strength.
I know God has reasons
For every life's length.

I'm sorry to say that I didn't give it much attention or discuss it with him, so I never knew, at the time, what prompted such serious thoughts. But a few months after he died, as I was reading those words through bitter tears, it hit me like a thunderbolt - Teddy had written this as a message to me! With unerring prescience he knew that someday I would need to hear him say, "Pops, I love you, and I want you to go on living, not weakened by my loss, but strengthened by the love we share. Your life has meaning, and I'm part of that meaning. Let your memories of me make your life better. Remember, I know God has reasons for every life's length!"

How does a 14-year-old boy realize so deep and fundamental a truth, one that most of us never grasp until we're hit over the head with it? I don't know. But I did learn, from one short poem, that love cannot be caged by a mere span of years.

Thank you, God, for a son whose life was as loving and beautiful as it was short.

> Herbert A. Tiedemann
> Father of Teddy
> Born 9/24/63
> Died 10/10/79

GOD KNOWS WHAT'S BEST FOR ME, MOM

Have I not commanded thee? Be strong and of a good courage; be not afraid, neither be thou dismayed: for the Lord thy God is with thee withersoever thou goest.

Joshua 1:9 (KJV)

Cancer! No word stirs the soul of man with as much dread - not even Hell itself.

"Barbara will be dead in 6 weeks," we were told. The words stung with unbearable pain, an ever-increasing pain that endured for five years and taught our family of six what it means to "trust" in the Lord and lean on Him for strength.

Our pain was emotional; Barbara's was both physical and mental, but it didn't defeat her. She didn't want to die, but she wasn't afraid. (The verse quoted above gave her courage.) Although she was 13 when the cancer was diagnosed, her outlook was that of a mature adult who had led a long life and is ready to give it up. The disease caused her to grow up quickly; she by-passed those glorious teen-aged years.

Bit by bit her illness deprived her of the ability to function "on her own." She was unable to swallow her saliva, breathe or eat, yet she never complained and never blamed God. Near the end of her struggle "to make it" and win the battle to live, she told me, "If I were to ask the Devil to make me well, I know he would, but I would rather die trusting Jesus, who made me, to know what is best for me."

Like her, we believe there is a time to be born and a time to die and that when God's time comes, the "healers" of this world can't change the plan He has for your life.

Barbara's death showed us how short life can be and made us aware of how long eternity is. She was with us here for just a few short years but we can live with that, knowing that in the next life we'll be together forever.

Dear Lord, thank you for your promise of eternal life and the joy of knowing that one day we'll be reunited with our loved ones who have gone before us.

Dorothy Walker
Mother of Barbara
Born 1/7/59
Died 9/19/77

BRIGHT SUNSHINE AND BUTTERFLIES

I go to prepare a place for you.
John 14:2 (KJV)

I keep crying over Peggie's empty apartment and remembering the final-feeling that came with dismantling it. Her apartment - her own creation, was an extension of all that was Margaret Ann Woodson.

She'd always loved bright, cheery things and so had decorated her bedroom all in yellow. The walls, the drapes, the bedspread merged in one blaze of sunshine. And her butterfly craze? Well, you could not count the many-splendored, winged creatures that lighted in those rooms.

"I want to go back to my apartment, Mother," she said to me in the hospital. And as hope grew more wistful, just "I love my apartment." I make myself remember something else Peggie said to me in the hospital, after the first time she had been critical. "A picture dropped into my mind last week, Mother, an oval picture like you'd find in an old-fashioned fairy tale book, only smudged around the edges. A cameo of bright sunshine and butterflies and meadow flowers. It was so vivid, Mother, when everything else in my mind was so blurred, do you think it was given to me as a picture of heaven?"

Dear God, bright sunshine and butterflies.

Then, too, I make myself remember Joe, my husband, sitting beside Peggie's bed reading to her again and again the words of Jesus: "In my father's house are many rooms. I go to prepare a place for you." Joe always emphasized the *for you.* "You know how you love your apartment, Peggie? How you've fixed it up so it reflects your tastes and desires? Well, if you die, you'll still have your own place, Peg, a place fixed up by Jesus just *for you.*"

I keep reminding myself that Peggie's apartment is an *empty tomb*, for Peggie has moved into an apartment in heaven reflective of a Peggie Woodson she had scarcely dreamed could be.

Yes, I think your cameo was given to you, Peggie. And to me.

Please, God, let me be true to my sorrow, but let me also be thankful for all the Peggie-happiness Peggie is experiencing now in Your apartment complex.

Meg Woodson
Mother of Margaret Ann
Born 3/12/60
Died 6/6/83

JEFF'S LEGACY

The measure of a life, after all, is not its duration, but its donation.
                                        Peter Marshall

People used to tell Jeff that he smiled so much because it showed off his dimples. Nonetheless, it was impossible not to be affected by his easy-going charm and constant good humor.

His life ended abruptly at the age of 24, on a highway 600 miles from home. The effect was overwhelming and almost immediate.

From all over the country they came - friends of his, friends of his siblings - flying, driving, hitchhiking - from college campuses and new jobs. They overflowed our home, the funeral parlor and the church. Literally a thousand people sent messages - some had known Jeff but not us, some had known us but not Jeff, and some had known neither but were somehow touched by it all. It was as if the hand of God had reached down and picked up these hundreds and hundreds of people, shook them up a little, and then set them down facing a new direction.

We were fortunate. In the excruciating pain of our loss we never felt a need to ask "why?" It was so obvious that the positive force of this loving young man was intensified by the fact that nothing he had ever done could be repeated or rescinded. If he had lived another 80 years, he could not have touched more people than he did by dying.

The frality of our tenuous hold on a span of time on this planet is always accentuated by the sudden death of someone so young and so alive. Friends and acquaintances told us of estranged families reuniting, of religious faith rekindled, of a reassessment of priorities - all because of this incident. That is Jeff's legacy, and I suspect it is the unwritten legacy of all our children.

Dear God, thank you for letting us see the little miracles of good which spring from even the darkest tragedies.

                        Abigail Sammon
                        Mother of Jeffrey
                        Born 8/30/58
                        Died 10/20/82

YOUR CHILD IS WAITING

Yet Yahweh's love for those who fear him lasts from all eternity and for ever, like his goodness to their children's children.
Psalms 103:17 (TJB)

Two days after a wonderful family Thanksgiving, our 28-year-old daughter took her own life.

Heidi was a beautiful, brilliant, sensitive young woman, but her days were filled with tragedies. She was raped, her marriage didn't last, and she suffered anorexia nervosa. During a low ebb she decided to escape this world and join the Lord she had served since childhood in the next.

We are a close family, and the horror of her suicide overwhelmed us. "Did she shut herself out of heaven" I wondered, "because she took her own life, or is she really there?" That nagging fear became a tormenting thought that plagued me and I cried to the Lord for an answer.

I was awakened one night and received the assurance I sought as He spoke in my heart. This is what He said.

"Your child is waiting here to welcome you.

She was eager and restless to be gone from there.

Here she knows she should have waited for my perfect choice, but she alone is to know My will and fate that could have been. My grace is great and let her in.

She isn't sad any more. In my face she sees the Father's love she wanted there below.

Be comforted. Turn aside your grief and be ready once again to shine. Someday you will see well the meaning of the loss. The time is short so be alive in me."

Praise you, Lord, that you spoke into our darkness and despair and brought peace and hope.

Muriel Hall
Mother of Heidi
Born 9/17/54
Died 11/28/82

THE WAY OUT

We pray you will be strengthened from God's glorious power, so that you may be able to pass through any experience and endure it with joy.

Colossians 1:11 (ME-P)

My husband, our two little boys and I had eagerly anticipated the arrival of our new baby; preparations had been made, names chosen - and suddenly, all of our expectations and dreams were no more. When a newborn dies, not only are the memories few, but specific hopes for that child must be written off.

Since Russell just lived a few hours, my husband and I and the medical personnel involved were the only people who saw him. It was difficult for our family and friends who hadn't spent any time with him to understand the magnitude of our loss. Because they were unable to identify with our situation, our only source of consistent strength and support was God.

I turned to books on healing grief and to the Bible for help. Ironically, some of the scriptures that I thought would be most comforting were difficult to understand in light of what had happened. Or at least they were until something or someone shed a new light on their meaning.

The verse quoted above is an example. Knowing that "endure" means "to tolerate, or to bear pain," I wondered if that meant that I was to bear the pain of losing our child with joy? How could I do that? I certainly wasn't glad that my son was dead.

Then one day a comment I'd read in John Claypool's book TRACKS OF A FELLOW STRUGGLER flashed across my mind. He, who has also lost a child, said that the only way out of this indescribable pain is the way of gratitude. Life is a gift. The proper response to any gift is one of gratitude. If that gift, for whatever reason, is taken away, our response should be one of gratefulness for the time it was ours - regardless of the brevity of that time.

Russell lived a few hours, but even if he had died in my womb he would still have had a relationship with me while I nutured him, and for that gift I will always be grateful.

Dear Lord, help me to rely on your strength, and experience your joy in all that I may encounter in life.

Susan Simon
Mother of Russell
Born 6/5/82
Died 6/5/82

SIMPLY HEALING

. . . in his favor is life: weeping may endure for a night, but joy cometh in the morning.

Psalms 30:5 (KJV)

Tim's brothers were home for the holidays, and together we took another step in the long process of recovery. All of Tim's personal possessions had, for the past three years, been kept in a big box in the attic. Together we sorted and separated the contents until it all lay in sad piles and each item had been laid claim to or marked for disposal. Others would have done this much sooner, but I couldn't. One of the first lessons I learned about grief is that the only timetable that is right is the timetable that is right for me.

I have sometimes felt guilty that I wanted to move away from pain, to start reweaving the unraveled stands of my life, and I've wondered what Tim would say about that. Would he think I was forgetting him or that I was trying to be rid of him?

For a long, long time, on my way to and from work, I drove past the place where he died. I could have gone an alternate route if I had wanted to, but it became part of my day to glance into those trees at the scene of the accident, looking for what I don't know. Even at night I looked up the dark lane, despite the fact I couldn't see a thing. That was my ritual until one night I realized I had driven a half mile past before I remembered where I was. I had forgotten to look, and for a while the guilt I felt was heartbreaking.

Then gradually I came to realize that I wasn't forgetting him at all. I was just beginning to stop clinging to the thoughts and routines that I used to keep my grief alive and fresh. Now I occasionally go another way to town, and I can do so without feeling a nagging little guilt. I have also started to allow my mind to take advantage of the natural healing power that we all have, if we will let ourselves use it.

I am not losing or forgetting Tim. I am simply healing.

Lord, when tears and sorrow come to perch on my shoulder, as they sometimes do, let me remember that one joyous morning my child and I will be reunited.

Judy Dickey
Mother of Tim Hughes
Born 8/31/54
Died 7/20/79

WE HEAL BECAUSE WE HAVE BEEN WOUNDED

He will wipe away every tear from their eyes, and death shall be no more, neither shall there be mourning nor crying nor pain any more, for the former things have passed away.
Revelations 21:4 (RSV)

As a chaplain in a large hospital in Indianapolis, Indiana, I had seen death many times, and sometimes it was my responsibility to break that news to the loved ones. Each time the knot of fear clutched at my heart and the anguish tore me apart as I stood and gently prayed with and for the persons involved, and yes, sometimes I even cried with them.

When I had learned to conquer my own emotions sufficiently, I set up workshops to help bereaved parents deal with the pain and loss that was theirs. And I learned many things from them, too.

During one of those workshops a woman rose and began to talk with the persons present. She told them that although they were her friends, none had mentioned the name of her little daughter since her death. Then she burst into tears and told them that although she might cry when they mentioned her child's name, she needed to cry and she needed to talk about her daughter. "In this way," she told them, "I know you won't forget her."

And then it happened. The young woman I was sharing an apartment with was killed instantly in an accident on her way home from Christmas vacation. Although I had lectured many times about grief-related feelings and how to respond to someone in pain, I had never experienced those emotions myself.

For weeks I walked in a daze, too emotionally drained to think clearly. Over and over I repeated to myself Psalm 23 - The Lord is my Shepherd. Only then did I realize fully what Father Henri Nouwen meant when he talked (in his book by that title) about "The Wounded Healer" and how we are able to heal because we have been wounded.

Thank you, God, for shepherding me through the wounded time so that I might become a healer for others.

Sister Catherine Livers

68

REACH OUT AND HELP YOURSELF

Praise be to the God and Father of our Lord Jesus Christ, the Father of compassion and the God of all comfort, who comforts us in all our troubles, so that we can comfort those in any trouble with the comfort we ourselves have received from God.
2 Corinthians 1:3-4 (NIV)

You who have endured the stinging experiences are the choicest counselor God can use.
Chuck Swindoll

On February 4, 1977, I stepped out of our car holding our healthy 8-week-old daughter, Kristine. A few seconds later, I held her once again, dead in my arms after she was killed instantly when our car rolled backwards and struck us, dealing a fatal blow to her head.

Grief involves a struggle through many negative feelings. But eventually the time comes when the choice is ours as to what we do with what has happened. We have no choice about our child's death, but we can choose whether we want to be bitter and angry, or whether to grow and find a positive experience.

The cross was once a symbol of ugliness, a slow, painful way of death for criminals. Surely this seemed a defeat - the most negative event that could happen to a person claimed to be the Son of God, holy and sinless. But that cross has been turned from something negative into something positive - a symbol of hope for a major world religion.

My daughter's death seemed so senseless, a waste; the difference between life and death a matter of seconds and a thousand "if onlys." No person's life, no matter how short, or their death, is in vain or without meaning. Because Kristine lived and because she died, my life will be forever affected. To remain bitter and unhappy would be destructive to me and the meaning of her life. One of the secrets to healing is that, in helping others, you help yourself. God works through people; we are His hands and feet.

My choice is to use my suffering and hurt to reach out in understanding and compassion to others who are also hurting. What is yours?

Thank you, Lord, for being able to use our negative experiences for something good.

Pat Haas
Mother of Kristine
Born 12/10/76
Died 2/4/77

ALWAYS LAST WEEK

To every thing there is a season, and a time to every purpose under heaven: A time to be born, and a time to die . . . A time to weep, and a time to laugh; a time to mourn, and a time to dance . . . He hath made everything beautiful in his time . . . I know that there is no good in them, but for a man to rejoice, and to do good in his life.
Ecclesiastes, 3: 1-2, 4, 11, 12 (KJV)

Dear Matthew,

Today is July 27, ten years to the day since you left us. I went to the cemetery after work. Mom left a beautiful red rose and a bit of fern from our backyard in front of your marker.

Ten years seems like a long time, and yet, when I look at the pictures, it seems like just last week that we went camping and swimming at the reservoir. Indeed I think it will always be just last week.

I don't have anything really important to tell you, other than that Mom and Mark and I love you. You are still with us in our hearts and minds. Even though we miss you, the hurt and the ache are gone (except occasionally), and we can look back on our years with you as among the best we have ever lived. We know that in God's great scheme of things, we'll be together again, and we look forward to that.

Until then, we've learned to not say goodbye, but hello and hello and hello. May this day every year, and all days, be days for us to laugh and dance and rejoice and do good. The time for dying and weeping and mourning is past.

Dear little Matthew, I love you very much.

Your Dad

Dennis Douglass
Father of Matthew
Born 10/22/71
Died 7/27/73

Please send me the following books:

_____ copies of **MEDITATIONS FOR
BEREAVED PARENTS** @ $6.95 each = $ _____

_____ copies of **MEDITATIONS FOR THE
WIDOWED** @ $6.95 each = $ _____

_____ copies of **MEDITATIONS FOR THE
DIVORCED** @ $6.95 each = $ _____

_____ copies of **MEDITATIONS FOR THE
TERMINALLY ILL AND THEIR
FAMILIES** @ $6.95 each = $ _____

_____ copies of **MEDITATIONS FOR
ALCOHOLICS AND THEIR
FAMILIES** @ $6.95 each = $ _____

SUBTOTAL $ _____

For orders of 10 or more books, subtract 10%. $ _____

Add $1.50 shipping costs for the first book and
.25 cents for each additional book to the same address. $ _____

Add $1.50 for each additional shipping address. $ _____

(Gilgal will include a gift card in
each shipment to a separate address.)

TOTAL DUE $ _____._____

Call (503) 593-8418 to place VISA or MasterCard orders.

Ship to: Name _____

Address _____

City/State/Zip _____

Gift Address

Ship to: Name _____

Address _____

City/State/Zip _____

Name of sender for gift card_____

Mail order form to: Gilgal Publications
P.O. Box 3399
Sunriver, OR 97707 USA